HEROES FOR YOUNG READERS
ACTIVITY GUIDE
FOR BOOKS 1–4

Gladys Aylward • Eric Liddell
Nate Saint • George Müller

Renee Taft Meloche

YWAM
PUBLISHING
P.O. BOX 55787 SEATTLE, WA 98155

YWAM Publishing is the publishing ministry of Youth With A Mission. Youth With A Mission (YWAM) is an international missionary organization of Christians from many denominations dedicated to presenting Jesus Christ to this generation. To this end, YWAM has focused its efforts in three main areas: (1) training and equipping believers for their part in fulfilling the Great Commission (Matthew 28:19), (2) personal evangelism, and (3) mercy ministry (medical and relief work).

For a free catalog of books and materials, contact:

YWAM Publishing
P.O. Box 55787, Seattle, WA 98155
(425) 771-1153 or (800) 922-2143
www.ywampublishing.com

Heroes for Young Readers Activity Guide for Books 1–4
Copyright © 2005 by Renee Taft Meloche

10 09 08 07 06 05   10 9 8 7 6 5 4 3 2 1

Published by Youth With A Mission Publishing
P.O. Box 55787
Seattle, WA 98155

ISBN 1-57658-367-8 (10-digit)
ISBN 978-1-57658-367-8 (13-digit)

Printed in the United States of America.

Contents

Introduction

This activity guide is designed to accompany the following books from the Heroes for Young Readers series by Renee Taft Meloche and Bryan Pollard: *Gladys Aylward: Daring to Trust; Eric Liddell: Running for a Higher Prize; Nate Saint: Heavenbound*; and *George Müller: Faith to Feed Ten Thousand*. It provides the Christian schoolteacher, Sunday-school teacher, and homeschooling parent with ways to teach and reinforce the important lessons of these books.

Each book contains the following parts:

- ❖ **Coloring Page.** There is a picture of each hero with memorable people and events surrounding him or her for the children to color.
- ❖ **Hero Song.** The hero song is a tool to reinforce the main lesson of the hero. Music is often more memorable than spoken or written text.
- ❖ **Character Quality.** Each hero is given a character quality for the children to focus on. Discussion questions and visual aids are provided.
- ❖ **Character Activity.** The character activity uses drama or arts and crafts to convey more fully the character quality of the hero.
- ❖ **Character Song.** The character song encourages children to develop the particular character quality in their own lives.
- ❖ **Shoebox Activity.** This activity uses arts and crafts to create a keepsake to remember each hero and how they served. The children will put this keepsake into a shoebox (or other container) so that they will have a treasure box of memories of the heroes.
- ❖ **Cultural Page.** This page illustrates something that is representative of the country each hero worked in as a missionary, such as an animal, game, craft, or recipe.
- ❖ **Map.** The map page, which the children will color, shows the country or countries the hero lived in growing up and as a missionary.
- ❖ **Flag.** A flag (usually of the country the hero worked in as a missionary) is provided for the children to color.
- ❖ **Fact Quiz.** This page tests the children's comprehension of each hero story by giving true and false statements inside a particular object that relates to that story. The children will color in the true statements and draw an X over the false statements.
- ❖ **Fun with Rhyme.** This page has five stanzas from each hero story. The last word of each stanza is blank, and the children try to fill in the blank, rhyming it with the last word in the second line. A Word Bank is provided for very young readers. (When making copies, the Word Bank can be covered up for the more advanced reader and speller.)
- ❖ **Crossword Puzzle.** This page tests the children's comprehension of each story. A Word Bank is provided for young readers. (Again, when making copies, the Word Bank can be covered up.)

❖ **Can You Name the Hero?** This exercise has four stanzas, each providing clues about a hero. The children guess which hero each stanza is about.

Before you begin this activity guide, you may want to highlight which activities best suit your needs. For instance, a Sunday-school teacher might want to focus on the coloring pages, songs, character activities, and shoebox activities, while a schoolteacher might want to focus more on the crossword puzzle, fact, map, and cultural pages. A thirteen-week syllabus is included at the end of this activity guide for those parents and teachers who would like a guide to covering some or all of the activities.

Reinforcing stories with fun and creative illustrations, songs, drama, and arts and crafts brings the heroes to life and helps the children remember the important lessons learned through the lives of heroes—ordinary men and women who did extraordinary things with God.

Gladys Aylward: Daring to Trust

Gladys Aylward Song

Gladys went to China where the children's feet were bound. She freed them from their bindings so they could run around.

When China was attacked and had to enter into war, Gladys gathered children without parents, ninety-four.

In China, in China, brave Gladys went to China, and led them over mountain trails; with God she could not fail.

In China, in China, brave Gladys went to China. With God as her great strength and guide, she saved the children's lives.

The Good Character Quality
of Gladys Aylward

Definition of Perseverance: Never giving up no matter how hard it gets.

Bible Verse: "Let us run with perseverance the race marked out for us" (Hebrews 12:1).

Materials

❖ Copy of the crown, strip, and diamond jewel labeled "perseverance" on page 12 for each child (use heavy white paper or card stock; if you do not wish to have the children color their crowns, use heavy yellow paper or yellow card stock)
❖ Scissors
❖ Crayons or colored pencils
❖ Stapler
❖ Tape or glue

Steps to Follow

1. Introduce the character quality of perseverance, which describes Gladys, and discuss its meaning with the children. Read aloud the Bible verse above.

2. Have the children color and cut out the diamond labeled "perseverance." (Because it is a diamond, tell them they may want to leave the middle part white.)

3. Have the children color and cut out their crown and strip. Read aloud the following scripture verse: "Now there is in store for me the crown of righteousness, which the Lord, the righteous Judge, will award to me on that day" (2 Timothy 4:8).

4. Have the children tape or glue the diamond to the crown. Then have them staple the strip to the crown and put it around their heads. The crown will serve as their "thinking cap" about perseverance.

5. Ask the children, "How did Gladys show perseverance in her life through her words or actions?"
   ❖ Even though she failed Bible college and did not speak much Chinese, she did not give up her dream of becoming a missionary to China. She went there anyway and learned the language.

❖ When Gladys took the children over the mountains of China, she did not give up but kept going until she and the children made it safely to an orphanage.

6. Ask the children if they know someone—a parent, neighbor, or friend—who demonstrates perseverance in their lives. Have them tell the class about this person.

7. Ask the children to think of examples in their own lives when they have persevered or where they would like to persevere more, such as:
   ❖ Learning a difficult piano piece
   ❖ Training for a race
   ❖ Studying for a hard math test

8. Have the children sing the character song "We Will Persevere" on page 13. (This song is sung to the tune of "Do Your Ears Hang Low?" and is also included with the character activity for Gladys on page 14. If you have the CD for Gladys Aylward, you can have the children follow or sing along with this song. At the end of the CD, there is a solo piano accompaniment, which the children can sing along with as well.)

Note: This activity carries over into all the hero stories that follow. For each hero, there will be a new character quality inside a different jewel. You can have the children keep adding jewels to the crowns that they've already made or have them make new crowns each time this activity is repeated. Please be aware that the jewels are a fun way to reinforce the lesson, not a suggestion that the children should expect to be rewarded for doing the right thing as Christians.

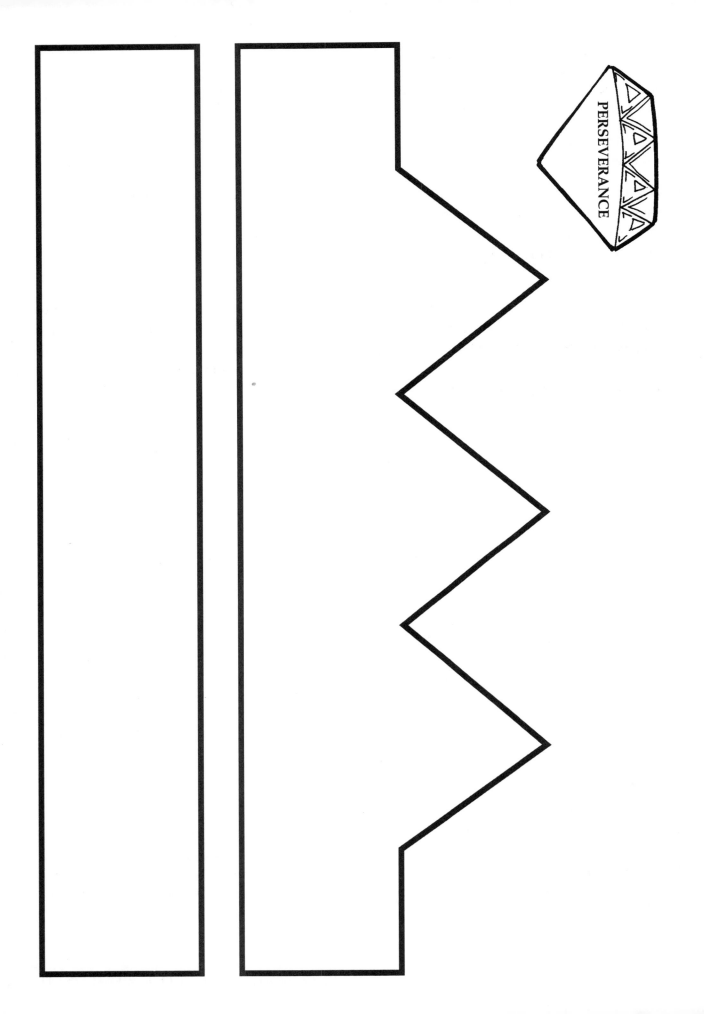

PERSEVERANCE

Gladys Aylward Character Song

We Will Persevere

We will per-se-vere. We will ne-ver, ne-ver quit. We will
fol - low God and we will stick to it. We will not give up, not one
sin - gle lit - tle bit. We will per - se - vere.

Character Activity for Gladys Aylward

An Imaginary Journey Across the Mountains of China

1. Tell the children, "We're going to go on our own journey across the mountains of China. You're the orphans, and I'm Gladys Aylward. First, let's all lie on the ground and pretend to be asleep." (You should have a large space cleared of tables and chairs.)

2. "Okay, now wake up, children. Let's stretch our arms and rub our eyes." (Demonstrate this to them.)

3. "We have a long journey ahead of us, so here's a little rice for each of you." (Pantomime giving the children a small amount of rice.) "It isn't much, but I know God will provide more for us when we need it."

4. Begin walking, and have the children follow. "Be careful of the rocky ground. Ow!" (Gladys grabs her foot and hobbles. Some of the other children groan as well.) "It's okay. We'll be all right. We must just keep on going."

5. "Look at the beautiful flowers." (Pretend to pick one and encourage the others to do so.) "My flower is bright yellow. What are the colors of your flowers?" (Several students yell out their colors.) "If God can provide for these flowers to grow up so strong and beautiful, surely He will give us the strength to make it to the orphanage."

6. "Oh no! A large log has come crashing down in front of us. We must get across. You older children, please help the little ones jump over it." (Demonstrate taking a child's arm and helping him or her jump over it.)

7. "Okay, now let's keep walking. I know it's hard for you little ones and for those of you whose feet were bound when young. But God will give us the strength to keep going."

8. "What was that?" (Look up in the sky.) "I think I hear some planes coming. Quick! Duck behind some trees!"

9. "They're gone now." (Breathe a sigh of relief.) "I know you're getting tired, but we must keep going. Let's sing a song to help lift our spirits." (Sing the character song "We Will Persevere" on page 13.)

10. "Look at the birds circling overhead! They're landing on our arms. My bird is bright red. What colors are your birds?" (Have several children yell out colors.) "Let's hold our birds close and whisper something special to them."

11. "God gives the birds strong wings to fly from place to place and provides the food they need to survive. Surely, if He will feed these birds, He will feed us and give us the strength to keep going if we don't give up."

12. "Let's say good-bye to our birds." (Lift your arm toward the sky and pretend to let the bird go.)

13. "Come on, children, let's keep moving. We have to climb through some prickly bushes now, so be careful of the thorns."

14. "I know we're all feeling pretty worn out now, but we must not quit. Look, we've come to a fork in the road. Let's see. We need to go southwest. By looking at the sun, I think we need to go to the left [or right, if easier]."

15. "We'll have to climb this hill that looks really steep, so watch your step. We can do it. Let's not give up. With God's help, I'm certain we can all make it to the orphanage—every single one of us."

16. "I know it's getting hotter, we're getting thirsty, and our mouths are dry. But look! I see a stream at the bottom of the hill. Be careful getting down. Don't slip! Some of you older children hold on to the little ones."

17. "Let's get down on our knees and cup our hands and drink from the stream. Let's see how nice the water feels on our faces and wash them."

18. "Now let's take our shoes off and wade across to the other side. Oh, the water feels so good on our feet."

19. "Let's keep going. It looks like the sun's going down. We need to find a place to sleep. Look over there; I see a cave. Let's get inside it for the night."

20. "Before we go to sleep, let's pray: Dear Lord, thank You for giving us the strength to make it on our journey so far. Help us to trust You so that we will keep going and never give up until we make it safely to the orphanage. Amen."

Shoebox Activity for Gladys Aylward
Looking at Good and Bad Behavior

Note to parents and teachers: A Shoebox Activity is included for each Christian hero in this activity guide. At the end of each missionary adventure that the children experience, the children will have keepsakes to put in their shoeboxes of memories. If you prefer, you may choose a different container in which the children can store their keepsakes.

Materials

- ❖ Three to five squares of paper for each student
- ❖ A large shoebox (with lid) that each student will bring in with his or her name on the bottom (decorating the outside is optional)
- ❖ A few large pictures that show good or bad behavior (photographs, magazine pictures, or simple drawings that show actions and expressions that illustrate good and bad behavior)
- ❖ Wastepaper basket

Steps to Follow

1. Tell the children, "You are going to draw or cut out some pictures that show good and bad behavior. Before you do, let's look at a few pictures that I have and decide whether they show good or bad behavior" (e.g., a girl sweeping the floor with a grumpy look on her face; a mother reading to her son; a father helping his son walk over some rough rocks; a little boy sharing his ice cream with his sister; sisters or brothers fighting).

2. After holding up these pictures one at a time and allowing the students to respond, pass out five pieces of paper to each child and tell them to draw five pictures that show good or bad behavior (e.g., two stick figures, with one helping the other one in some way or with one tripping another or making fun of another).

3. When the children have finished, demonstrate to them how they will sort their pictures. Place a shoebox in front of you and take off the lid. Pick up one of your pictures and, without talking, show by your expression whether the picture shows good or bad behavior. If it is a bad picture, place it next to your shoebox. If it is a good picture, place it inside your shoebox. Then tell the children, "Now you try it. I will be looking at your faces to see if I can tell what kind of pictures you are looking at."

4. Next, tell the children, "Pick up all of your bad pictures, stand up, and walk to the wastepaper basket and throw your pictures into it."

5. After they have returned to their places and sat down, tell them, "This is what God does when we do something wrong and ask His forgiveness. He gets rid of all the bad pictures in our lives and remembers them no more."

6. Tell the children to put the lids back on their shoeboxes, and then say, "I'm going to read a story about Christian hero Gladys Aylward. As I read, I want you to look at the pictures of her life and see what her pictures say about her."

7. After the children have heard the story, ask them, "What kind of a person do we see when we look at the pictures of Gladys Aylward?" Then ask, "What were some good things Gladys did?"
   ❖ She didn't quit.
   ❖ She praised God in difficult circumstances.
   ❖ She lived her life for God and others.

8. After the children have heard the story, tell them you will keep their shoeboxes with their good pictures in them until they listen to another missionary adventure and add something new to their box of memories.

Hand Counting

Materials

❖ Copy of the Chinese hand counting chart (see following page) for each child

Steps to Follow

1. Tell the children, "The Chinese marketplace can be very busy and crowded. Because it is often noisy, the Chinese have developed a way of showing the numbers one to ten with the fingers on just one hand so that they do not have to shout out the number of items they want to buy."

2. Using the Chinese hand counting chart as a guide, teach the children to count to ten by using the fingers on one hand.

3. Have the children answer the following questions by using the correct Chinese hand-counting positions:

   ❖ How many years had Gladys been in China before Japan invaded? (Answer: eight)
   ❖ How many Japanese airplanes appeared and dropped bombs on the Chinese village where Gladys lived? (Answer: five)
   ❖ How many soldiers heard the children singing on the riverbank of the Yellow River and offered to take them across in a wooden boat? (Answer: one)
   ❖ When the bridge to Sian was bombed, how many days did Gladys and the children have to walk to catch another train? (Answer: five)
   ❖ Tell the children: "Pretend you are orphans going over the mountains of China with Gladys. How old are you?" (Let all the children, one by one, answer this question.)
   ❖ See if the children can fill in the blank with the correct number from this rhyme from the Gladys Aylward book:

   As time went on, the children lost
   their parents to the war,
   so Gladys took the children. Soon
   they numbered ninety- _____.

   (Answer: four)

Chinese Hand Counting Chart

Map: Gladys Aylward

On the map, find England, where Gladys Aylward grew up, and color it in.

Now find China, where Gladys lived as a missionary, and color it in.

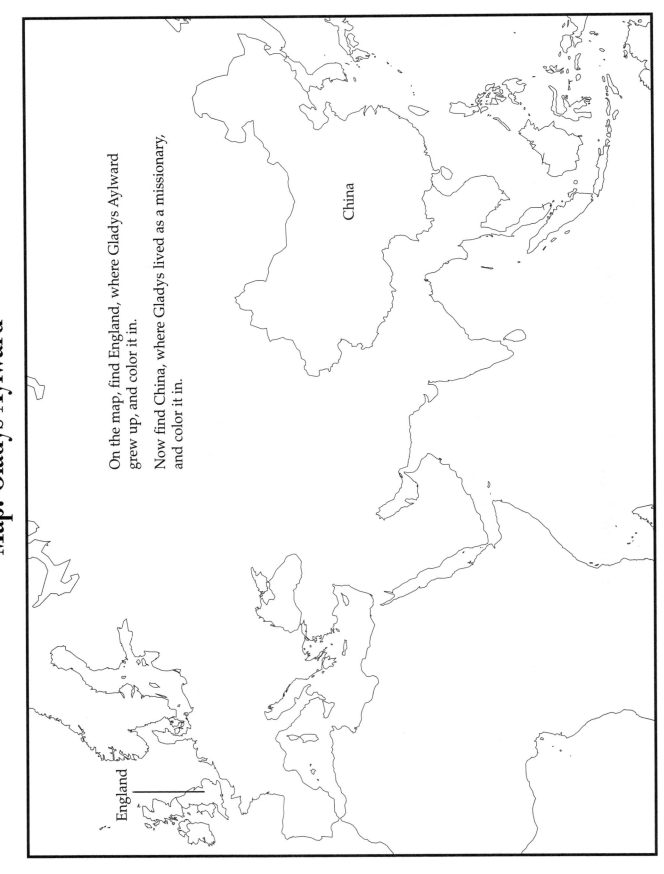

China

England

The Flag of China

Above is the flag of China. Color the stars yellow and the rest of the flag bright red.

Gladys Aylward Quiz

Color the boxcars whose facts are correct.
Draw a big X over the boxcars whose facts are incorrect.

Gladys grew up in England.

Today we can still trust God to provide for us.

The older girls limped over the mountains because they wore cheap shoes when they were young.

The coal dust kept the children safely hidden.

The government asked Gladys to be a foot inspector.

When the children escaped over the mountains, they slept at night in log cabins.

The Chinese thought big feet were beautiful.

When the children were tired, Gladys screamed at them to keep going.

Gladys spoke little Chinese when she arrived in China.

Gladys was an excellent student in Bible college.

Fun with Rhyme

It's your turn to be a poet. See if you can fill in the correct word inside each boxcar without looking at your book on Gladys Aylward. Hint: The word will rhyme with the last word in the second line.

Word Bank

four
free
late
guide
long
dark

She met a mother with a child
    of three upon her knee,
and said, "Unbind her bandages
    so that her feet are

As time went on the children lost
    their parents to the war,
so Gladys took the children. Soon
    they numbered ninety-

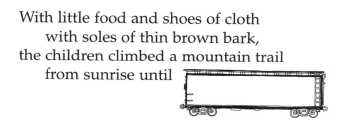

With little food and shoes of cloth
    with soles of thin brown bark,
the children climbed a mountain trail
    from sunrise until

The older girls all limped along.
    Their pain was very great
because the bindings on their feet
    had been removed too

So Gladys taught them hymns to sing
    to keep their spirits strong.
This cheered them some, and yet they knew
    the road ahead was

Like Gladys Aylward we today
    can trust God to provide
along our journey, through our lives,
    to be our faithful

Gladys Aylward Crossword Puzzle

Across

2. The town the orphans were going to.
3. The name of the river the orphans crossed.
6. The kind of train the children rode on.
9. How many orphans did Gladys rescue?
11. The kind of songs Gladys taught the orphans.
12. What country invaded China?

Down

1. Gladys told the Chinese what kind of stories?
4. What country did Gladys come from?
5. Gladys was what kind of inspector?
7. The number of children Gladys lost.
8. God still does what for us today?
10. Where was Gladys a missionary?

Eric Liddell: Running for a Higher Prize

Eric Liddell Song

Eric loved to run so much, he had a great big dream. He wanted to compete one day on the Olympic team.

He made the move, but Eric's race was on God's special day. Instead he chose to honor God and would not run—no way!

On Sunday, on Sunday, he would not run on Sunday. Though Eric had the fastest feet, he would not compete.

On Sunday, on Sunday, he would not run on Sunday. Though Eric would have won the race, he put God in first place.

The Good Character Quality
of Eric Liddell

Definition of Honorable: Having the courage to stand alone for what you believe is right.

Bible Verse: "My Father will honor the one who serves me" (John 12:26).

Materials

- ❖ Copy of the crown, strip, and emerald jewel labeled "honor" on page 30 for each child (use heavy white paper or card stock; if you do not wish to have the children color their crowns, use heavy yellow paper or yellow card stock)
- ❖ Scissors
- ❖ Crayons or colored pencils
- ❖ Stapler
- ❖ Tape or glue

Steps to Follow

1. Introduce the character quality of honor, which describes Eric, and discuss its meaning with the children. Read aloud the Bible verse above.

2. Have the children color and cut out the emerald labeled "honor." (Because it is an emerald, you may want to suggest they color it green.)

3. Have the children color and cut out the crown and strip. Read aloud the following Bible verse: "Do you not know that in a race all the runners run, but only one gets the prize? Run in such a way as to get the prize. Everyone who competes in the games goes into strict training. They do it to get a crown that will not last; but we do it to get a crown that will last forever" (1 Corinthians 9:24–25).

4. Have the children tape or glue the emerald to their crown. Then have them staple the strip to the crown and put it around their heads. The crown will serve as their "thinking cap" about honor.

5. Ask the children, "How did Eric honor God and others in his life through his words or actions?"

- ❖ He would not run on Sunday.
- ❖ He loaned his trowel to the other runners before a race.
- ❖ When people came to hear him talk about running, he also took the opportunity to tell them about God and His Son.
- ❖ He served the Chinese as a missionary.

6. Ask the children if they know someone—a parent, neighbor, or friend—who demonstrates honor to God and/or others in their lives. Have them tell the class about this person.

7. Ask the children what ways they can honor God in their lives, such as:
   - ❖ Obeying parents and teachers
   - ❖ Having a good attitude when doing chores
   - ❖ Showing good sportsmanship

8. Have the children sing the character song "We Will Honor God" on page 31. (This song is sung to the tune of "Do Your Ears Hang Low?" If you have the CD for Eric Liddell, you can have the children follow or sing along with this song. At the end of the CD, there is a solo piano accompaniment, which the children can sing along with as well.)

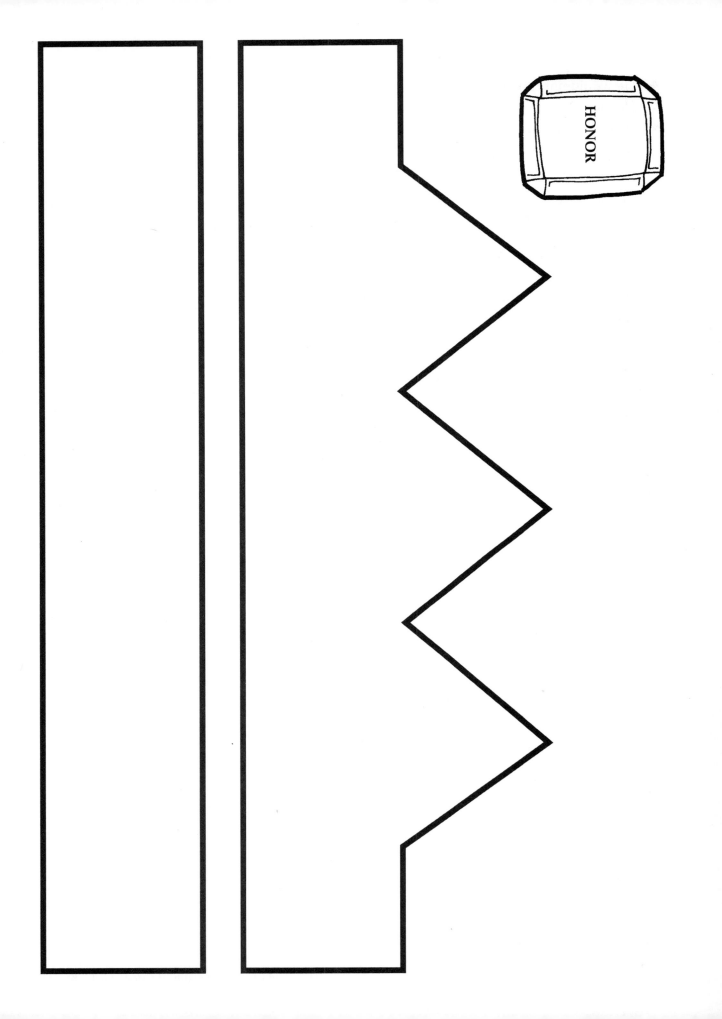

HONOR

Eric Liddell Character Song

We Will Honor God

We will ho - nor God. We will put God in first place. We will not do an - y-thing to bring dis - grace. We will be good sports, no mat - ter what the race. We will ho - nor God.

Character Activity for Eric Liddell

Showing Honorable and Dishonorable Sportsmanship

Steps to Follow

1. Pair each child with a partner: one becomes the sculptor, the other becomes the clay. Each sculptor must mold his or her "clay" partner into a statue that represents a person doing a sports action (e.g., hitting a baseball, diving, running). The sculptors must do this without speaking or even telling their partners what their sports action is. Have the sculptors first work on the body shape and then on the facial details (tell them to be gentle!).

2. When the statues are completed and are frozen, each statue must guess what sports action he or she is portraying.

3. Next, have the sculptors walk around observing the other statues, trying to guess what sports action each statue is portraying.

4. Now have sculptors return to their partners and reverse roles.

5. Have each pair combine with another pair to make a group of four. Ask the children, "If I were to take a picture of a sports scene showing good or bad sportsmanship, what would it look like?" (You may need to help them out by demonstrating a few examples, such as tripping another runner, sneering when someone wins, helping someone up when he or she falls, or shaking hands after a sports match.)

6. Tell each group which kind of sportsmanship you want them to demonstrate (good or bad). Then tell the group to think of a scene (let them talk it through this time), create it one by one, and then freeze. After a few minutes, have each group come up to the front of the class and form their scene. If time permits, have the groups switch and demonstrate the opposite kind of sportsmanship from their previous scene.

Shoebox Activity for Eric Liddell

Putting God First, Others Second, and Me Third

Materials

- ❖ Copy of three ribbons for each child (shown on the following page)
- ❖ Gold, silver, and bronze crayons

Steps to Follow

1. Have each child color the first ribbon gold, the second ribbon silver, and the third ribbon bronze. On the gold ribbon have them write 1st Place God; on the silver, 2nd Place Others; and on the bronze, 3rd Place Me:

2. Have each child cut out their gold, silver, and bronze ribbons.

3. When they have completed this assignment, have the children place their ribbons in their shoeboxes. This will serve as a reminder of how Eric put God first in his life and to encourage them to do likewise.

Scottish Foods

Below are some Scottish foods:

Shortbread	a kind of cookie
Scone	small biscuit-like pastry or bread
Sausage Roll	a roll made of highly seasoned pork or other meats
Porridge	cereal, like oatmeal
Salmon	a type of fish
Tablet	a small flat cake
Haddock	a type of fish
Grouse	a type of bird
Bannock	a pancake made of oatmeal, barley, or wheat flour

Now see if you can match these scrambled Scottish food words with the correctly spelled ones. Draw a line from the scrambled word to the correct word.

EURGOS	**SHORTBREAD**
DEGRIPOR	**SCONE**
OMASLN	**SAUSAGE ROLL**
CNNABOK	**PORRIDGE**
CKDDAHO	**SALMON**
EGSSAAU LORL	**TABLET**
TTLEBA	**HADDOCK**
ENOSC	**GROUSE**
HTROSBERAD	**BANNOCK**

Map: Eric Liddell

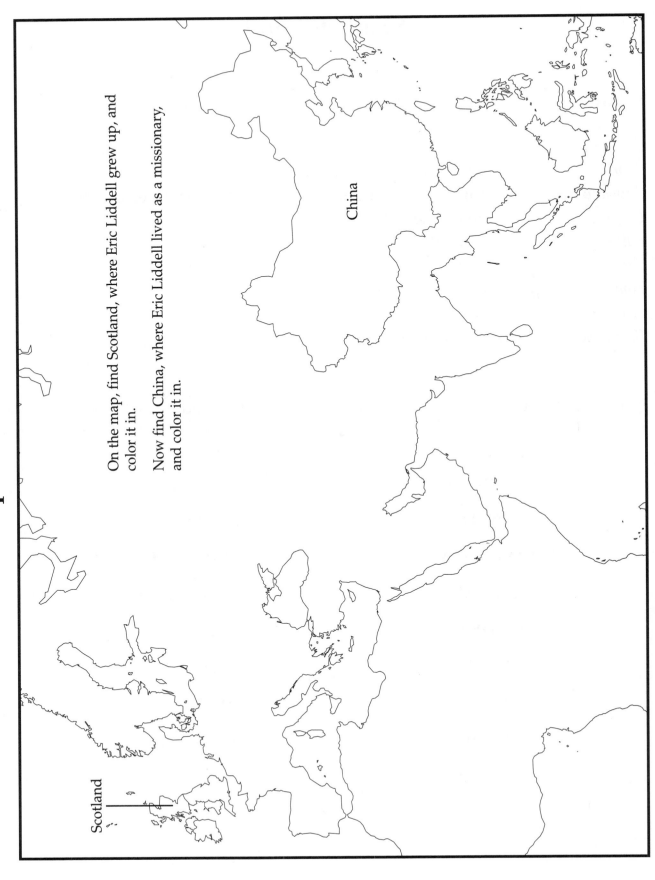

On the map, find Scotland, where Eric Liddell grew up, and color it in.

Now find China, where Eric Liddell lived as a missionary, and color it in.

China

Scotland

The Olympic Flag

Above is the Olympic flag. From the left, color the first ring blue, the second ring yellow, the third ring black, the fourth ring green, and the fifth ring red.

Eric Liddell Quiz

Color the shoes whose facts are correct.
Draw a big X over the shoes whose facts are incorrect.

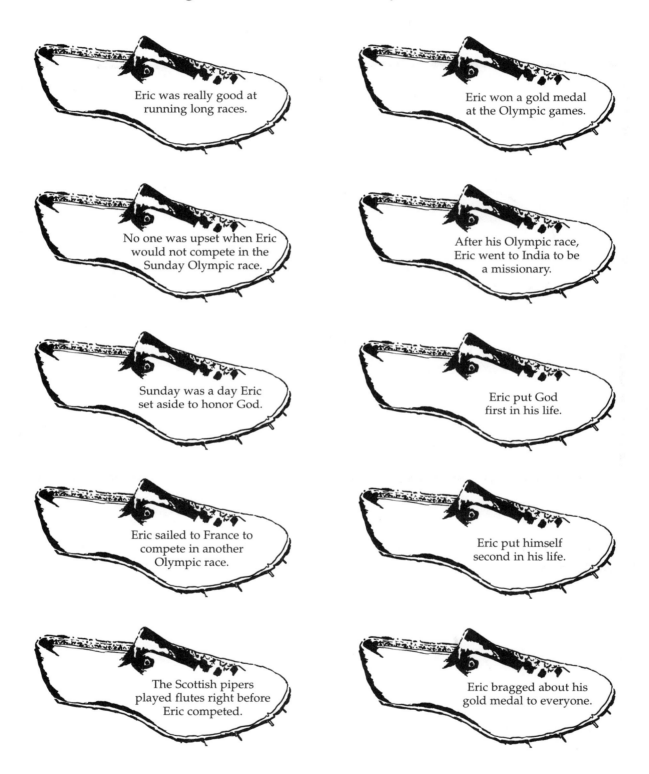

Eric was really good at running long races.

Eric won a gold medal at the Olympic games.

No one was upset when Eric would not compete in the Sunday Olympic race.

After his Olympic race, Eric went to India to be a missionary.

Sunday was a day Eric set aside to honor God.

Eric put God first in his life.

Eric sailed to France to compete in another Olympic race.

Eric put himself second in his life.

The Scottish pipers played flutes right before Eric competed.

Eric bragged about his gold medal to everyone.

Fun with Rhyme

It's your turn to be a poet. See if you can fill in the correct word inside each shoe without looking at your book on Eric Liddell. Hint: The word will rhyme with the last word in the second line.

Word Bank

grass
best
run
place
Son
feet

A Scottish boy named Eric Liddell
    thought the greatest fun
was moving fast just like the wind:
    he simply loved to

As he grew up, he soon became
    impossible to beat,
for he excelled in every sport;
    he had the fastest

When Eric raced the next week, though,
    a runner tried to pass,
and accidentally tripped him, knocking
    Eric to the

When people came to hear him talk
    of how he loved to run,
he also took the chance to speak
    about God and His

For Sunday was a day for God—
    to honor Him and rest.
He simply would not run that day,
    although he was the

And now he lives with God since he
    has finished this life's race,
and when he was a champion here
    he put God in first

Eric Liddell Crossword Puzzle

Word Bank

Olympic

China

Britain

rugby

God

Sunday

Scotland

four hundred*

honor

gold

*no space in crossword

Across

1. What kind of medal did Eric win?
5. "He who honors me, I will _ _ _ _ _."
7. Eric became a missionary in what country?
8. What country was Eric from?
9. Another sport Eric was good at.

Down

2. Eric's dream was to compete on the
   _ _ _ _ _ _ _ team.
3. How many meters was Eric's great race?
4. Something Eric loved more than running.
6. For what country did Eric compete?
8. On what day wouldn't Eric run?

Nate Saint: Heavenbound

Nate Saint Song

When Nate first had an airplane ride, he did not have a doubt that he'd become a pilot; it was all he talked about.

He learned to fly and bravely flew his airplane for the Lord in thick and deep, dark jungle in the land of Ecuador.

The airplane, the airplane, Nate loved to fly his airplane. The missionaries loved to hear Nate's airplane coming near.

The airplane, the airplane, Nate loved to fly his airplane. He used the plane to drop supplies and help save many lives.

The Good Character Quality
of Nate Saint

Definition of Helpfulness: Being useful and considerate of others.

Bible Verse: "Get Mark and bring him with you, because he is helpful to me in my ministry" (2 Timothy 4:11).

Materials

❖ Copy of the crown, strip, and ruby jewel labeled "helpfulness" on page 46 for each child (use heavy white paper or card stock; if you do not wish to have the children color their crowns, use heavy yellow paper or yellow card stock)
❖ Scissors
❖ Crayons or colored pencils
❖ Stapler
❖ Tape or glue

Steps to Follow

1. Introduce the character quality of helpfulness, which describes Nate, and discuss its meaning with the children. Read aloud the Bible verse above.

2. Have the children color and cut out the ruby labeled "helpfulness." (Because it is a ruby, tell them they may want to color it red.)

3. Have the children color and cut out the crown and strip. Read aloud the following Bible verse: "Be faithful ... and I will give you the crown of life" (Rev. 2:10).

4. Have the children tape or glue the ruby to the crown. Then have them staple the strip to the crown and put it around their heads. The crown will serve as their "thinking cap" about being helpful.

5. Ask the children, "How did Nate show helpfulness in his life through his actions?"
   ❖ He dropped supplies to the missionaries.
   ❖ He dropped gifts to the Indians.

6. Ask the children if they know someone—a parent, neighbor, or friend—who demonstrates helpfulness. Have them tell the class about this person.

7. Ask the children if they can think of ways that they can show helpfulness, such as:
   ❖ Clearing the dinner dishes off the table without being asked
   ❖ Offering to read or entertain a younger brother or sister
   ❖ Helping to bring in the groceries
   ❖ Helping to take out the garbage

8. Have the children sing the character song "We'll Show Helpfulness" on page 47. (This song is sung to the tune of "Do Your Ears Hang Low?" If you have the CD for Nate Saint, you can have the children follow or sing along with this song. At the end of the CD, there is a solo piano accompaniment, which the children can sing along with as well.)

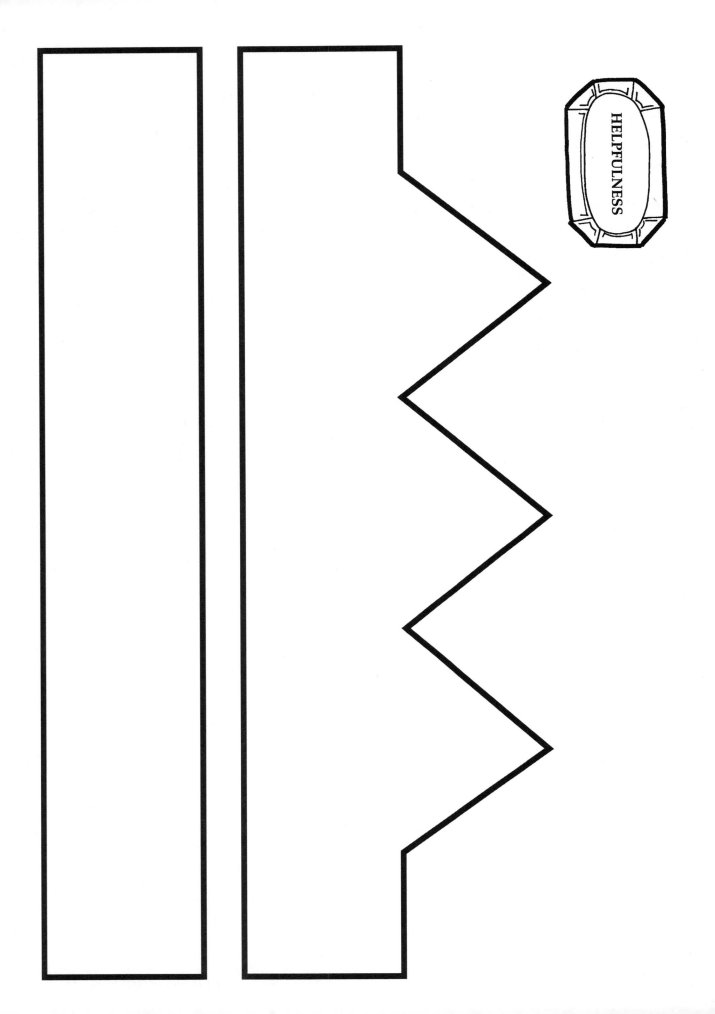

HELPFULNESS

Nate Saint Character Song

We'll Show Helpfulness

Character Activity for Nate Saint

Supplies for the Missionaries and Indians

Materials

- ❖ 8.5 x 11 inch white paper (at least one sheet for each child)
- ❖ Pens or pencils for writing

Steps to Follow

1. Tell the children they are going to pretend to be airplanes. Have the children spread out their arms and carefully fly around the room.

2. Now tell the children they are going to be biplanes with two sets of wings. This time—working in pairs—have all of the children spread out their arms and fly around the room, moving closely together with their partners, as they pretend to be biplanes.

3. Now have the children sit down. Ask them, "What are some of the items that Nate flew to the Auca Indians and the missionaries?"
   - ❖ Medicine
   - ❖ Telephone
   - ❖ Yo-yo
   - ❖ Harmonica
   - ❖ Machete
   - ❖ Balloons
   - ❖ Toys
   - ❖ Kettle

4. Ask the children to think of supplies that they might fly to the missionaries and the Aucas; then have them draw or write these supplies on a piece of white paper.

Note: This activity carries over into the Shoebox Activity on the following page.

Shoebox Activity for Nate Saint

Flying Supplies to the Missionaries and Indians

Materials

- ❖ White paper with missionary and Indian supplies drawn or written (see Character Activity on previous page)
- ❖ Copy of paper airplane instructions on the following page for each child
- ❖ Laundry basket
- ❖ Sign that says "Palm Beach" taped to a laundry basket

Steps to Follow

1. Have the children take their white pieces of paper with their missionary and Indian supplies drawn or written and make paper airplanes out of them, following the instructions on the following page.

2. Have the children try to land their planes in the laundry basket labeled "Palm Beach."

3. Have the children take their airplanes and put them in their shoeboxes to remind them of how Nate Saint used his airplane to help others.

Paper Airplane Instructions

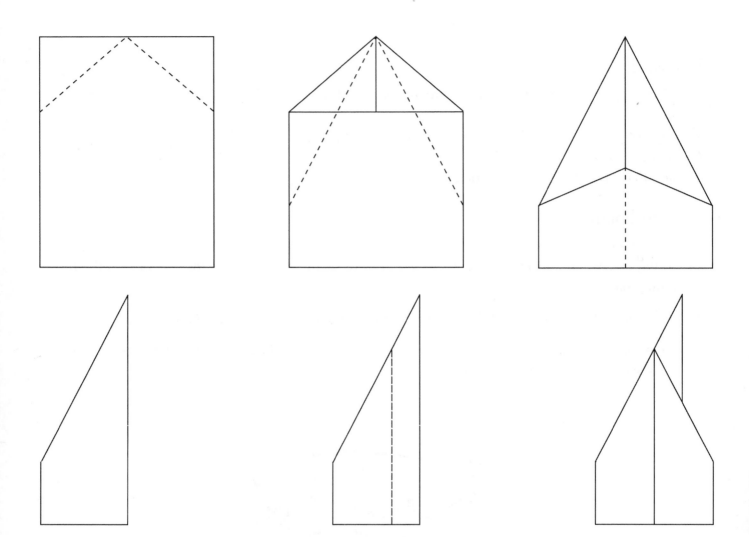

The Spider Monkeys of Ecuador

Spider monkeys live for about 25 years and are skinny animals with long arms and legs, which make them look like spiders. Like us, they are very active during the day and sleep during the night. They have humanlike fingers but do not have thumbs. They live in the tropical forests, where they eat fruit, leaves, nuts, eggs, seeds, and insects. They like to be high up, and as they swing from tree to tree, they make a loud barking noise. Although these animals may seem friendly, if people get too close, spider monkeys will pull their hair and grab their jewelry.

On the following page is a picture of a spider monkey. Color the monkey light brown and the tree limbs green or dark brown.

The Spider Monkey of Ecuador

Map: Nate Saint

Ecuador

South America

The country of Ecuador is about the size of the state of Colorado. Its streets are often crowded with horses, donkeys, bicycles, and carts.

Color the country of Ecuador red.

The capital city of Ecuador is Quito, close to where the Auca Indians live.

Write the word *Quito* next to the dot, which shows the city's location.

The Flag of Ecuador

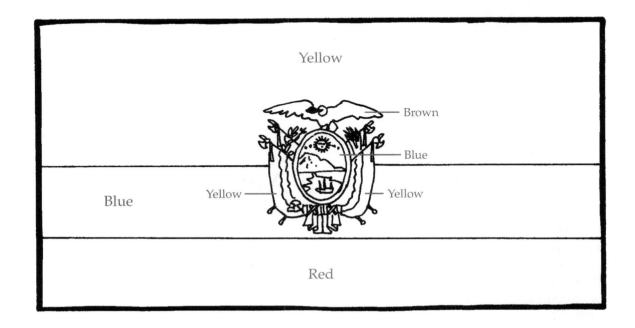

Above is the flag of Ecuador. Color the flag red, blue, yellow, and brown where indicated.

Nate Saint Quiz

Color the airplanes whose facts are correct.
Draw a big X over the airplanes whose facts are incorrect.

Nate wanted to be a fireman when he grew up.

Nate wanted to be a pilot who served God.

Nate stored his supplies in cylinders on the wings of his airplane.

Nate's sister, Rachel, refused to forgive the Indians who had killed her brother.

Nate dropped unfriendly letters to the Aucas from his airplane.

Nate was one of ten missionaries who were killed by the Aucas.

Six years after the missionaries were killed, not one Auca had become a Christian.

Nate used a parachute to drop supplies to the missionaries.

Nate wanted to let the Aucas know the good news about God's Son.

The Aucas killed the missionaries because they thought they had attacked George.

Fun with Rhyme

It's your turn to be a poet. See if you can fill in the correct word inside each airplane without looking at your book on Nate Saint. Hint: The word will rhyme with the last word in the second line.

Word Bank

sky
bird
done
ground
face
fight

He pulled back on the wheel and sent
    the airplane heavenbound.
He pushed it forward and the airplane's
    nose dipped toward the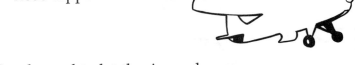

Nate longed to let the Aucas hear
    the good news of God's Son,
His message of forgiveness, and
    the great things He had

When priests or hunters or explorers
    came in day or night,
they often would be ambushed though
    they hadn't come to

But first Nate had to be their friend
    and thought that he would try
to drop gifts to the Aucas from
    the safety of the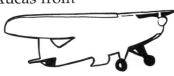

So Nate flew Ed and three more friends
    back to that sandy place.
They hoped to meet the Aucas and
    share God's love face to

Yet not one single Auca came.
    Instead each noise they heard
turned out to be some animal
    or squawking jungle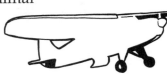

Nate Saint Crossword Puzzle

Word Bank

chaperone

forgiveness

Ecuador

spear

machete

biplane

warrior

primitive

Auca

martyr

Across

1. A large, heavy knife with a broad blade.
5. One who dies for his faith.
7. A simple dwelling or lifestyle.
8. Aircraft with two sets of wings at different levels.
10. The kind of weapon Nate was killed with.

Down

2. A person who accompanies young, unmarried women in public.
3. A country in South America.
4. One who fights in battles.
6. What Nate's sister showed the tribe.
9. An Indian name meaning "savage."

George Müller: Faith to Feed Ten Thousand

George Müller Song

George lived in England, where he rescued orphans off the streets. He started up a breakfast club and served oatmeal to eat.

George found a place where they could live. The orphans found it nice. For once they'd had to share their space with lots of rats and mice.

The orphans, the orphans, George loved the English orphans. He helped ten thousand orphans out that no one cared about.

The orphans, the orphans, George loved the English orphans. He showed God's love by caring for the children who were poor.

The Good Character Quality of George Müller

Definition of Faith: A strong belief and unshakable confidence in God.

Bible Verse: "If you have faith as small as a mustard seed, you can say to this mulberry tree, 'Be uprooted and planted in the sea,' and it will obey you" (Luke 17:6).

Materials

❖ Copy of the crown, strip, and opal jewel labeled "faith" on page 64 for each child (use heavy white paper or card stock; if you do not wish to have the children color their crowns, use heavy yellow paper or yellow card stock)
❖ Scissors
❖ Crayons or colored pencils
❖ Stapler
❖ Tape or glue

Steps to Follow

1. Introduce the character quality of faith, which describes George, and discuss its meaning with the children. Read aloud the Bible verse above.

2. Have the children color and cut out the opal labeled "faith." (Because it is an opal, tell them they may want to color it milky white or pastel.)

3. Have the children color and cut out the crown and strip. Read aloud the following Bible verse: "And when the Chief Shepherd appears, you will receive the crown of glory that will never fade away" (1 Peter 5:4).

4. Have the children tape or glue the opal to the crown. Then have them staple the strip to the crown and put it around their heads. This will serve as their "thinking cap" about faith.

5. Ask the children, "How did George show faith in his life through his words and actions?"
    ❖ He had faith that God would provide the money to build an orphanage.
    ❖ He had faith that God would provide for the needs of every orphan in his care.

❖ Even though there was no food for the orphans for breakfast, he prayed and thanked God for what they were about to eat.

6. Ask the children if they know someone—a parent, neighbor, or friend—who demonstrates faith in God in their lives. Have them tell the class about this person.

7. Have the children sing the character song "We Have Faith in God" on page 65. (This song is sung to the tune of "Do Your Ears Hang Low?" If you have the CD for George Müller, you can have the children follow or sing along with this song. At the end of the CD, there is a solo piano accompaniment, which the children can sing along with as well.)

FAITH

George Müller Character Song

We Have Faith in God

We will put our faith in our
God who al-ways cares. We'll be con-fi-dent— He will
an-swer prayer. We will put our faith in our
God who's al-ways there. We have faith in God.

Character Activity for George Müller

Reenacting the Breakfast Scene

Materials

- ❖ One or two long tables (depending on the number of children)
- ❖ Copies (cut out) of the shillings on page 68 (one for each child)
- ❖ Dinner rolls or mini muffins, baked and ready to eat (one for each child)
- ❖ Plate for the dinner rolls
- ❖ Small child-size cartons of milk (or orange juice) or one gallon of milk (or orange juice) and a plastic cup for each child
- ❖ Three pieces of paper with the following lines for George, the baker, and the milkman written out:

George: "Let's all please take a seat. Thank You, Lord, for giving us what we're about to eat."

Baker: "I could not sleep because I thought you'd need this bread today."

Milkman: "My cart has broken down outside. I've unloaded all my milk so I can fix it properly. Please take my milk and drink it now, for all my milk is free."

Steps to Follow

1. Have the children pretend to be orphans and walk around, demonstrating different emotions that you call out: loneliness, hunger, sadness, etc. Ask them to show what their faces would look like and how they would walk.

2. Have the orphans come across a bakery and look in the window, pressing their faces against it. Ask them how they would react to the smells and the sights of all those goodies.

3. Have the orphans look around in imaginary garbage cans and, finding nothing to eat, begin to dance on the streets to try to earn a shilling.

4. Pass out a shilling to each of the orphans for their dancing.

5. Have the orphans find the orphanage and have them gather around one or two long tables and reenact the breakfast scene in the George Müller book. Assign one child to be George, one to be a baker, and another to be a milkman, giving them the paper with their lines to read.

   a. While the orphans are standing and looking despondent, have George walk in and say, "Let's all please take a seat. Thank You, Lord, for giving us what we're about to eat."

   b. Next, the baker enters and says, "I could not sleep because I thought you'd need this bread today." Have the baker pass out the dinner rolls. Tell the children they can eat them.

c. Now the milkman enters and says, "My cart has broken down outside. I've unloaded all my milk so I can fix it properly. Please take my milk and drink it now, for all my milk is free." Have the milkman pass out the cartons or pour the milk.

6. This is a good opportunity to lead a discussion about the symbolism of bread in a Christian's life. Remind the children that every time we say the Lord's prayer, we ask God to "give us this day our daily bread" and that during communion we eat bread in memory of Jesus' life, death, and resurrection.

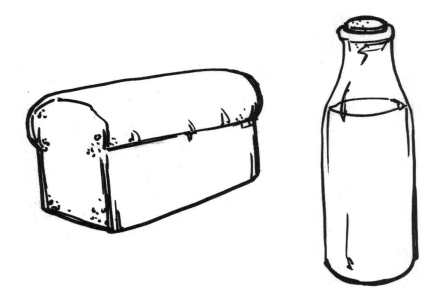

Shillings

Shoebox Activity for George Müller

Looking at Ways God Provides for Us

Materials

❖ A copy of either the girl or boy "orphan" pictures (printed on the next two pages) on heavy white paper or card stock (one for each child)

❖ Pens or pencils

❖ Yellow, brown, and black yarn

❖ Crayons or colored pencils

❖ Scissors

❖ Glue

Steps to Follow

1. Have the children take their girl or boy orphan pictures and write down or draw things on their pictures that God provides for us (e.g., food, shelter, friends, parents).

2. Have the children add eyes, noses, and mouths to their pictures.

3. Have them color the bodies of their orphans, explaining that they need to color lightly or color around the words or drawings that they have done.

4. Have the children use scissors to cut out their pictures.

5. Have the children glue on a few strands of yarn for the hair.

6. Have the children put their orphan pictures into their shoeboxes to remind them of how God provided for George and the orphans.

Orphan Boy

Orphan Girl

Schultüte Craft

George Müller was born and raised in the country of Germany. In Germany, children are often frightened when entering the first grade and don't have a lot of faith that things will go well. To make it easier for them, they are given a gift on the first day of school—a large, decorated paper cone called a Schultüte (SHOOL-tu-tuh). The Schultüte is filled with pencils, candy, and small gifts.

Materials

- ❖ 11-inch card stock square (one for each child)
- ❖ Tissue paper
- ❖ Treats for stuffing the Schultüte
- ❖ 12-inch ribbon or yarn
- ❖ Colored pencils, crayons, markers, or puff paints
- ❖ Stapler
- ❖ White glue
- ❖ Tape
- ❖ Scissors

Steps to Follow

1. Fold the card stock in half diagonally.

2. Measure down the fold 4 inches and make a mark.

3. Draw a curved line from the outer corner to the mark on the fold.

4. With the card stock still folded, cut along the curved line from the outer corner to the mark on the fold.

5. Unfold the card stock and decorate one side (which will become the outside), using colored pencils, crayons, markers, or paint.

6. Roll the card stock into a cone shape and staple or tape the edge.

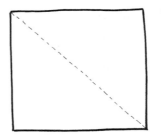
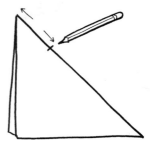
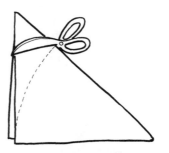

7. Line the inside of the cone with tissue paper, leaving enough tissue sticking up above the cone to be able to tie it shut.

8. Fill the cone with treats.

9. Gather the tissue paper together in the center and tie it closed with ribbon or yarn.

Map: George Müller

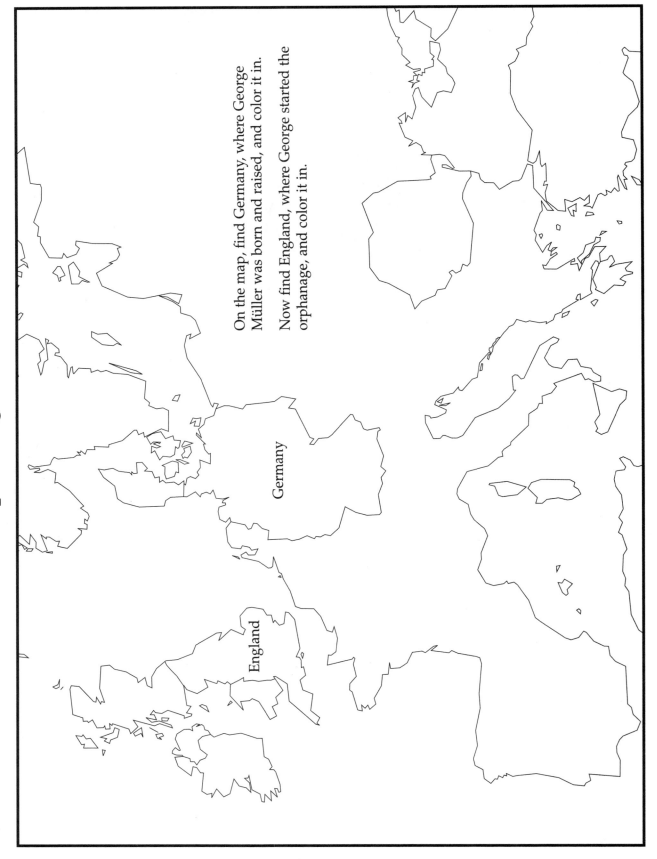

On the map, find Germany, where George Müller was born and raised, and color it in.

Now find England, where George started the orphanage, and color it in.

Germany

England

The Flag of England

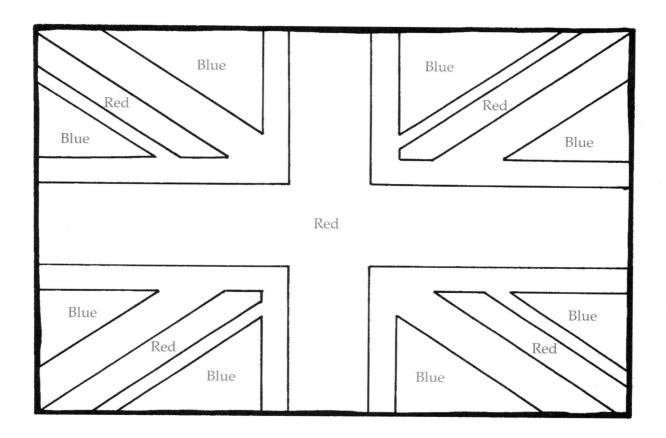

Above is the flag of England. Color the flag red and blue where indicated.

George Müller Quiz

Color the bread loaves whose facts are correct.
Draw a big X over the bread loaves whose facts are incorrect.

George was born and
raised in England.

Whenever George was
short of money, he spent
all his time worrying.

George wanted to
travel overseas to learn
new languages.

George often told the
orphans Bible stories.

George started a breakfast
club for the orphans.

God provided breakfast
through the milkman
and the baker in answer
to the children's
prayers.

George went to all his
friends and family and
begged them for the
money to start an
orphanage.

George gave William a
Bible when he left the
orphanage.

Some church people
thought God had more
important things than
the orphans to care
about.

George helped ten thousand
orphans during his life.

Fun with Rhyme

It's your turn to be a poet. See if you can fill in the correct word inside each bread loaf without looking at your book on George Müller. Hint: The word will rhyme with the last word in the second line.

Word Bank

care
ways
day
eat
lice
sight

He pushed past Bristol's poorest part
    along the cobbled street.
He hardly saw the beggars who
    were wanting food to

A baby boy named William had
    been born one morning there.
His parents died when he was small,
    yet no one seemed to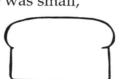

Wherever little William went
    there scurried rats and mice.
At night he hardly slept a wink—
    his bed had fleas and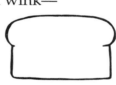

Now William was a boy of twelve
    when he came there to stay.
So strange at first, it felt to him
    more like his home each

George placed a coin in his left palm,
    a Bible in his right.
"Hold tightly to God's Word," he said.
    "Don't let it out of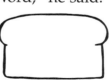

As George grew old, he settled down
    and spent his final days
surrounded by new orphans he
    could help in many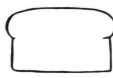

George Müller Crossword Puzzle

Word Bank

Bible

orphanage

pastor

England

helpful

shilling

prayed

ten thousand*

Prussia

poorhouse

*no space in crossword

Across

2. Be _ _ _ _ _ _ where you are.
4. What did William become when he grew up?
6. People with no money lived here.
8. George came from this country, now part of Germany.
9. In what country did George help the orphans?
10. A place for children with no parents.

Down

1. How many orphans did George help over the years?
3. God's holy Word.
5. What did George do when there was no breakfast?
7. A British coin.

Can You Name the Hero?

See if you can write the correct name of each hero in the space provided from the clues in each stanza.

Can you name the hero who bravely flew his plane
    for the Lord in Ecuador, over thick terrain?
Can you name this man who often dropped supplies
    by parachute to missionaries, saving many lives?

    His name was _____. He flew his plane for God.

Can you name the hero who helped the orphans out,
    ten thousand English orphans whom no one cared about?
Can you name this German who helped give food to eat
    to many English orphans whom he rescued off the streets?

    His name was _____. He helped the orphans out.

Can you name the hero who had the fastest feet,
    who entered the Olympics but then would not compete?
Can you name this Scotsman who would have won the race
    but since it was on Sunday chose to put God in first place?

    His name was _____. He put God in first place.

Can you name the hero who saved the children's lives,
    escaping over mountains with God as her great guide?
Can you name this woman who, during China's war,
    rescued many children? They numbered ninety-four.

    Her name was _____. She saved the children's lives.

Note: This exercise can also be sung by following along on the companion CD for books 1–4. When the chorus is repeated the second time, the answers are included.

Answers to "Can You Name the Hero?"

1. Nate Saint

2. George Müller

3. Eric Liddell

4. Gladys Aylward

Answers to Questions

Answers to Gladys Aylward

Gladys Aylward Quiz: Correct Facts

- ❖ Gladys grew up in England.
- ❖ Today we can still trust God to provide for us.
- ❖ The coal dust kept the children safely hidden.
- ❖ The government asked Gladys to be a foot inspector.
- ❖ Gladys spoke little Chinese when she arrived in China.

Fun with Rhyme

1. free
2. four
3. dark
4. late
5. long
6. guide

Crossword

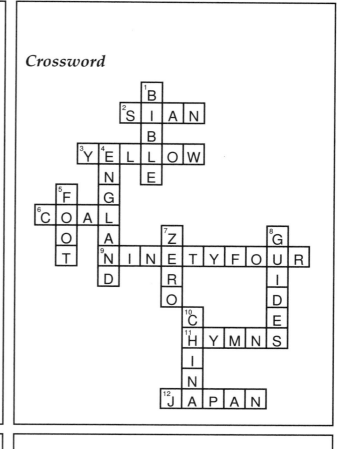

Answers to Eric Liddell

Eric Liddell Quiz: Correct Facts

- ❖ Eric won a gold medal at the Olympic games.
- ❖ Sunday was a day Eric set aside to honor God.
- ❖ Eric put God first in his life.
- ❖ Eric sailed to France to compete in another Olympic race.

Fun with Rhyme

1. run
2. feet
3. grass
4. Son
5. best
6. place

Crossword

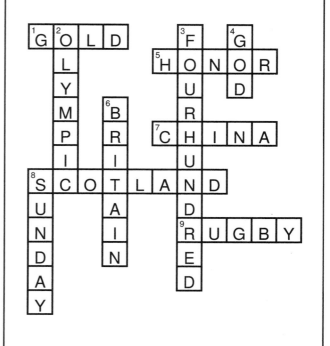

Answers to Nate Saint

Nate Saint Quiz: Correct Facts

- ❖ Nate wanted to be a pilot who served God.
- ❖ Nate stored his supplies in cylinders on the wings of his airplane.
- ❖ Nate used a parachute to drop supplies to the missionaries.
- ❖ Nate wanted to let the Aucas know the good news about God's Son.
- ❖ The Aucas killed the missionaries because they thought they had attacked George.

Fun with Rhyme

1. ground
2. done
3. fight
4. sky
5. face
6. bird

Crossword

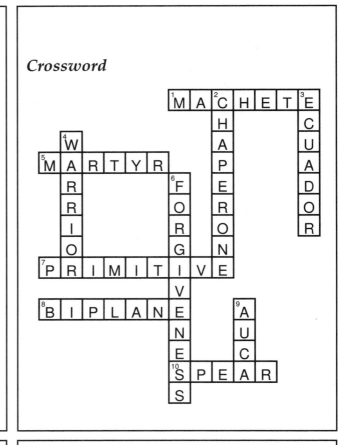

Answers to George Müller

George Müller Quiz: Correct Facts

- ❖ George was born and raised in England.
- ❖ George often told the orphans Bible stories.
- ❖ George started a breakfast club for the orphans.
- ❖ God provided breakfast through the milkman and the baker in answer to the children's prayers.
- ❖ George gave William a Bible when he left the orphanage.
- ❖ Some church people thought God had more important things than the orphans to care about.
- ❖ George helped ten thousand orphans during his life.

Fun with Rhyme

1. eat	3. lice	5. sight
2. care	4. day	6. ways

Crossword

I Will Follow

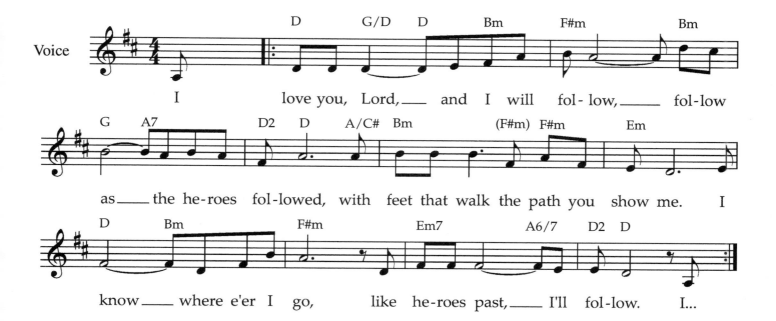

2. I love You, Lord, and I will follow,
    follow as the heroes followed,
    with hands that help in ways You guide me.
    I know where e'er I go,
    like heroes past, I'll follow.

3. I love You, Lord, and I will follow,
    follow as the heroes followed,
    with ears that hear the truth You tell me.
    I know where e'er I go,
    like heroes past, I'll follow.

4. I love You, Lord, and I will follow,
    follow as the heroes followed,
    with eyes that see the needs around me.
    I know where e'er I go,
    like heroes past, I'll follow.

Syllabus

Week 1

Gladys Aylward: 30-minute Class

1. Do the Shoebox Activity on pages 16 and 17, in the middle of which you'll read the book *Gladys Aylward: Daring to Trust* (25 minutes).
2. Learn and sing the "Gladys Aylward Song" by listening to the companion CD and following along on page 9 (5 minutes).

Gladys Aylward: 45-minute Class

1. Do the Shoebox Activity on pages 16 and 17, in the middle of which you'll read the book *Gladys Aylward: Daring to Trust* (25 minutes).
2. Learn and sing the "Gladys Aylward Song" by listening to the companion CD and following along on page 9 (5 minutes).
3. Take the Gladys Aylward Quiz on page 22 (5 minutes).
4. Color the map and flag on pages 20 and 21 (10 minutes).
   Optional: While the children are coloring, play the "Gladys Aylward Song," "We Will Persevere," and "I Will Follow" from the companion CD for them to listen to.

Week 2

Gladys Aylward: 30-minute Class

1. Learn about the Good Character Quality of Gladys on pages 10 and 11 (15 minutes) and sing the Character Song "We Will Persevere" on page 13 (5 minutes).
2. Enact the Character Activity on pages 14 and 15 (10 minutes).

Gladys Aylward: 45-minute Class

1. Review the "Gladys Aylward Song" on page 9 (5 minutes).
2. Do Fun with Rhyme on page 23 (5 minutes).
3. Learn about the Good Character Quality of Gladys on pages 10 and 11 (15 minutes) and sing the Character Song "We Will Persevere" on page 13 (5 minutes).
4. Enact the Character Activity on pages 14 and 15 (10 minutes).
5. Learn and sing the Prayer Song "I Will Follow" by listening to the companion CD and following along on page 83 (5 minutes).

Week 3

Eric Liddell: 30-minute Class

1. Read the book *Eric Liddell: Running for a Higher Prize* (10 minutes).
2. Sing the "Eric Liddell Song" by listening to the companion CD and following along on page 27 (5 minutes).
3. Do the Character Activity on page 32 (15 minutes).

Eric Liddell: 45-minute Class

1. Read the book *Eric Liddell: Running for a Higher Prize*. Tell the children to listen carefully because there will be a short quiz afterward (10 minutes).
2. Take the Eric Liddell Quiz on page 38 (5 minutes).
3. Sing the "Eric Liddell Song" by listening to the companion CD and following along on page 27 (5 minutes).
4. Do Fun with Rhyme on page 39 (5 minutes).
5. Do the Character Activity on page 32 (20 minutes).

Week 4

Eric Liddell: 30-minute Class

1. Learn about the Good Character Quality of Eric on pages 28 and 29 (10 minutes) and sing the Character Song "We Will Honor God" on page 31 (5 minutes).
2. Do the Shoebox Activity on pages 33 and 34 (10 minutes).
   Optional: While the children are coloring and cutting out their ribbons, play the "Eric Liddell Song," "We Will Honor God," and "I Will Follow" from the companion CD for them to listen to.
3. Review the "Eric Liddell Song" on page 27 (5 minutes).

Eric Liddell: 45-minute Class

1. Review the "Eric Liddell Song" on page 27 (5 minutes).
2. Learn about the Good Character Quality of Eric on pages 28 and 29 (10 minutes) and sing the Character Song "We Will Honor God" on page 31 (5 minutes).
3. Do the Shoebox Activity on pages 33 and 34 (10 minutes).
   Optional: While the children are coloring, play the "Eric Liddell Song," "We Will Honor God," and "I Will Follow" from the companion CD for them to listen to.
4. Learn about Scottish Foods and try to unscramble the words on page 35 (10 minutes).
5. Sing the Prayer Song "I Will Follow" by listening to the companion CD and following along on page 83 (5 minutes).

Week 5

Nate Saint: 30-minute Class

1. Read the book *Nate Saint: Heavenbound* (10 minutes).
2. Do the Character Activity on page 48 (10 minutes).
3. Do the Shoebox Activity on pages 49 and 50 (10 minutes).

Nate Saint: 45-minute Class

1. Read the book *Nate Saint: Heavenbound*. Tell the children to listen carefully because there will be a short quiz afterward (10 minutes).
2. Take the Nate Saint Quiz on page 55 (5 minutes).
3. Learn and sing the "Nate Saint Song" by listening to the companion CD and following along on page 43 (5 minutes).
4. Do Fun with Rhyme on page 56 (5 minutes).
5. Do the Character Activity on page 48 (10 minutes).
6. Do the Shoebox Activity on page 49 and 50 (10 minutes).

Week 6

Nate Saint: 30-minute Class

1. Learn and sing the "Nate Saint Song" by listening to the companion CD and following along on page 43 (5 minutes).
2. Take the Nate Saint Quiz on page 55 (5 minutes).
3. Learn about the Good Character Quality of Nate on pages 44 and 45 (10 minutes) and sing the Character Song "We'll Show Helpfulness" on page 47 (5 minutes).
4. Sing the Prayer Song "I Will Follow" by listening to the companion CD and following along on page 83 (5 minutes).

Nate Saint: 45-minute Class

1. Review the "Nate Saint Song" on page 43 (5 minutes).
2. Learn about the Good Character Quality of Nate on pages 44 and 45 (10 minutes) and sing the Character Song "We'll Show Helpfulness" on page 47 (5 minutes).
3. Repeat the Shoebox Activity on page 49 using the planes created from the previous week or make new ones (10 minutes).
4. Color the map and flag of Ecuador on pages 53 and 54 (10 minutes).
   Optional: While the children are coloring, play the "Nate Saint Song," "We'll Show Helpfulness," and "I Will Follow" from the companion CD for them to listen to.
5. Sing the Prayer Song "I Will Follow" by listening to the companion CD and following along on page 83 (5 minutes).

Week 7

George Müller: 30-minute Class

1. Read the book *George Müller: Faith to Feed Ten Thousand* (10 minutes).
2. Learn and sing the "George Müller Song" by listening to the companion CD and following along on page 61 (5 minutes).
3. Enact the Character Activity on pages 66 and 67 (15 minutes).

George Müller: 45-Minute Class

1. Read the book *George Müller: Faith to Feed Ten Thousand*. Tell the children to listen carefully because there will be a short quiz afterward (10 minutes).
2. Take the George Müller Quiz on page 76 (5 minutes).
3. Learn and sing the "George Müller Song" by listening to the companion CD and following along on page 61 (5 minutes).
4. Do Fun with Rhyme on page 77 (5 minutes).
5. Enact the Character Activity on page 66 and 67 (15 minutes).
6. Sing the Character Song "We Have Faith in God" on page 65 (5 minutes).

Week 8

George Müller: 30-minute Class

1. Learn about the Good Character Quality of George on pages 62 and 63 (10 minutes) and sing the Character Song "We Have Faith in God" on page 65 (5 minutes).
2. Do the Shoebox Activity on pages 69–71 (15 minutes).
   Optional: While the children are doing their craft, play the "George Müller Song," "We Have Faith in God," and "I Will Follow" from the CD for them to listen to.

George Müller: 45-Minute Class

1. Review the "George Müller Song" on page 61 (5 minutes).
2. Learn about the Good Character Quality of George on pages 62 and 63 (10 minutes) and sing the Character Song "We Have Faith in God" on page 65 (5 minutes).
3. Do the Shoebox Activity on pages 69–71 (15 minutes).
   Optional: While the children are doing their craft, play the "George Müller Song," "We Have Faith in God," and "I Will Follow" from the CD for them to listen to.
4. Color the map and flag on pages 74 and 75 (5 minutes).
5. Sing the Prayer Song "I Will Follow" on page 83 (5 minutes).

Week 9

Gladys Aylward: 30-minute Class

1. Reread the book *Gladys Aylward: Daring to Trust*. Tell the children to listen carefully because there will be a short quiz afterward (10 minutes).
2. Take the Gladys Aylward Quiz on page 22 (5 minutes).
3. Do the Chinese Hand Counting activity on pages 18 and 19 (5 minutes).
4. Color the Gladys Aylward picture on page 7 (10 minutes).
   Optional: While the children are coloring, play the "Gladys Aylward Song," "We Will Persevere," and "I Will Follow" from the CD for them to listen to.

Gladys Aylward: 45-Minute Class

1. Reread the book *Gladys Aylward: Daring to Trust*. Tell the children to listen carefully because there will be some questions during the next activity (10 minutes).
2. Do the Chinese Hand Counting activity on pages 18 and 19 (10 minutes).
3. Work the Crossword Puzzle on page 24 (10 minutes).
   Please note: For very young children, sing the "Gladys Aylward Song" on page 9, "We Will Persevere" on page 13, and "I Will Follow" on page 83 instead of doing the crossword puzzle.
4. Color the Gladys Aylward picture on page 7 (10 minutes).
   Optional: While the children are coloring, play the "Gladys Aylward Song," "We Will Persevere," and "I Will Follow" from the companion CD for them to listen to.
5. Review the "Gladys Aylward Song" on page 9 and/or "I Will Follow" on page 83 (5 minutes).

Week 10

Eric Liddell: 30-Minute Class

1. Reread the book *Eric Liddell: Running for a Higher Prize*. Tell the children to listen carefully because there will be a short quiz afterward (10 minutes).
2. Take the Eric Liddell Quiz on page 38 (5 minutes).
3. Color the Eric Liddell picture on page 25 (15 minutes).
   Optional: While the children are coloring, play the "Eric Liddell Song," "We Will Honor God," and "I Will Follow" from the CD for them to listen to.

Eric Liddell: 45-Minute Class

1. Reread the book *Eric Liddell: Running for a Higher Prize*. Tell the children to listen carefully because there will be a crossword puzzle afterward (10 minutes).
2. Work the Crossword Puzzle on page 40 (10 minutes).
   Please note: For very young children, sing the "Eric Liddell Song" on page 27, "We Will Honor God" on page 31, and "I Will Follow" on page 83 instead of working the crossword puzzle.
3. Color the map and Olympic flag on pages 36 and 37 (10 minutes).

4. Color the Eric Liddell picture on page 25 (10 minutes).

   Optional: While the children are coloring, play the "Eric Liddell Song," "We Will Honor God," and "I Will Follow" from the CD for them to listen to.

5. Review the Prayer Song "I Will Follow" on page 83 (5 minutes).

Week 11

Nate Saint: 30-Minute Class

1. Reread the book *Nate Saint: Heavenbound*. Tell the children to listen carefully because there will be a crossword puzzle afterward (10 minutes).
2. Work the Crossword Puzzle on page 57 (10 minutes).

   Please note: For very young children, sing the "Nate Saint Song" on page 43, "We'll Show Helpfulness" on page 47, and "I Will Follow" on page 83 instead of working the crossword puzzle.

3. Color the Nate Saint picture on page 41 (10 minutes).

   Optional: While the children are coloring, play the "Nate Saint Song," "We'll Show Helpfulness," and "I Will Follow" from the CD for them to listen to.

Nate Saint: 45-Minute Class

1. Reread the book *Nate Saint: Heavenbound*. Tell the children to listen carefully because there will be a crossword puzzle afterward (10 minutes).
2. Work the Crossword Puzzle on page 57 (10 minutes).

   Please note: For very young children, sing the "Nate Saint Song" on page 43, "We'll Show Helpfulness" on page 47, and "I Will Follow" on page 83 instead of working the crossword puzzle.

3. Learn about and color the Spider Monkeys of Ecuador on pages 51 and 52 (10 minutes).
4. Color the Nate Saint picture on page 41 (10 minutes).

   Optional: While the children are coloring, play the "Nate Saint Song," "We'll Show Helpfulness," and "I Will Follow" from the companion CD for them to listen to.

5. Review the "Nate Saint Song" on page 43 (5 minutes).

Week 12

George Müller: 30-Minute Class

1. Reread the book *George Müller: Faith to Feed Ten Thousand*. Tell the children to listen carefully because there will be a short quiz afterward (10 minutes).
2. Take the George Müller Quiz on page 76 (5 minutes).
3. Review the "George Müller Song" on page 61 (5 minutes).
4. Color the George Müller picture on page 59 (10 minutes).

   Optional: While the children are coloring, play the "George Müller Song," "We Have Faith in God," and "I Will Follow" from the companion CD for them to listen to.

George Müller: 45-Minute Class

1. Reread the book *George Müller: Faith to Feed Ten Thousand*. Tell the children to listen carefully because there will be a crossword puzzle afterward (10 minutes).
2. Work the Crossword Puzzle on page 78 (10 minutes).
   Please note: For very young children, sing the "George Müller Song" on page 61 and "We Have Faith in God" on page 65 instead of working the crossword puzzle.
3. Make the German Schultüte craft on pages 72 and 73 (15 minutes).
4. Color the George Müller picture on page 59 (10 minutes).
   Optional: While the children are coloring, play the "George Müller Song," "We Have Faith in God," and "I Will Follow" from the companion CD for them to.

Week 13

30-minute Class

1. Sing the song "Can You Name the Hero?" by listening to the companion CD and following along on page 79 (5 minutes).
2. Read the definitions of the character traits on each of the Good Character Quality pages and see if the children can guess the trait and the name of the hero that the trait applies to (5 minutes).
3. Play the game "Who Am I?" Have each child pick the name of one of the four heroes from a basket and give a clue about who that hero is. Let the rest of the class try to guess who the hero is (10 minutes).
4. Have each child pick the name of one of the four heroes from a basket and draw a picture that makes others think of that hero, e.g., a plane, running shoe, or bread loaf (10 minutes).

45-minute Class

1. Sing the song "Can You Name the Hero?" by listening to the companion CD and following along on page 79 (5 minutes).
2. Read the definitions of the character traits on each of the Good Character Quality pages and see if the children can guess the trait and the name of the hero that the trait applies to (5 minutes).
3. Play the game "Who Am I?" Have each child pick the name of one of the four heroes from a basket and give a clue about who that hero is. Let the rest of the class try to guess who the hero is (10 minutes).
4. Have each child pick the name of one of the four heroes from a basket and draw a picture that makes others think of that hero, e.g., a plane, running shoe, or bread loaf (10 minutes).
5. Tell who your favorite hero is and why (5 minutes).
6. Ask the children to pick their favorite songs and sing them (10 minutes).

Notes

Notes

Notes

Notes

Heroes for Young Readers

Written by Renee Taft Meloche • Illustrated by Bryan Pollard

Don't miss the exciting stories of other Christian heroes! Whether reading for themselves or being read to, children love the captivating rhyming text and unforgettable color illustrations of the Heroes for Young Readers series. See the next page for more activity guides and CDs.

BOOKS 1–4

Gladys Aylward: Daring to Trust • Trust in God enabled Gladys Aylward (1902–1970) to safely lead nearly one hundred Chinese orphans on a daring journey that saved their lives. ISBN 1-57658-228-0

Nate Saint: Heavenbound • Nate Saint (1923–1956) flew his plane over the jungles of Ecuador, helping missionaries reach isolated Indians with God's great love. ISBN 1-57658-229-9

Eric Liddell: Running for a Higher Prize • From winning Olympic gold as a runner to leaving his fame in Scotland behind to go to China as a missionary, Eric Liddell (1902–1945) put God in first place. ISBN 1-57658-230-2

George Müller: Faith to Feed Ten Thousand • George Müller (1805–1898) opened an orphanage, trusting God to faithfully provide for the needs of thousands of England's orphaned children. ISBN 1-57658-232-9

BOOKS 5–8

Corrie ten Boom: Shining in the Darkness • Corrie ten Boom (1892–1983) and her family risked everything to extend God's hand of love and protection to their Jewish neighbors during WWII. ISBN 1-57658-231-0

Amy Carmichael: Rescuing the Children • Amy Carmichael (1867–1951) rescued hundreds of women and children, first in Irish slums and then in India, by fearing God and nothing else. ISBN 1-57658-233-7

Mary Slessor: Courage in Africa • Mary Slessor (1848–1915) courageously shared Jesus' life and freedom with the unreached tribes of Africa's Calabar region. ISBN 1-57658-237-X

William Carey: Bearer of Good News • William Carey (1761–1834) left England behind and sailed to faraway India, where he devoted himself to translating the Bible into the native languages. ISBN 1-57658-236-1

BOOKS 9–12

Hudson Taylor: Friend of China • Known as one of the greatest pioneer missionaries of all time, Hudson Taylor (1832–1905) overcame huge obstacles to reach the Chinese. ISBN 1-57658-234-5

David Livingstone: Courageous Explorer • Trailblazing explorer David Livingstone (1813–1873) would not let anything stand in his way as he mapped unexplored Africa and healed the sick. ISBN 1-57658-238-8

Adoniram Judson: A Grand Purpose • Even imprisonment could not stop America's first foreign missionary, Adoniram Judson (1788–1850), as he translated the Bible into Burmese. ISBN 1-57658-240-X

Betty Greene: Flying High • Betty Greene (1920–1997) combined her love of flying with her love for Christ by helping found the Mission Aviation Fellowship. ISBN 1-57658-239-6

BOOKS 13–16

Lottie Moon: A Generous Offering • As a missionary to some of the poorest cities in China, once-wealthy Lottie Moon (1840–1912) experienced having nothing to eat. In dire circumstances, Lottie's first priority was teaching others about God's love. ISBN 1-57658-243-4

Jim Elliot: A Light for God • Jim Elliot (1927–1956) bravely faced both the wonders and the dangers of the South American jungle to share God's love with the feared and isolated Auca people. ISBN 1-57658-235-3

Jonathan Goforth: Never Give Up • In faraway China, despite danger and ridicule, Jonathan Goforth (1859–1936) and his wife generously opened their home to thousands of Chinese visitors, sharing the Good News of the gospel. ISBN 1-57658-242-6

Cameron Townsend: Planting God's Word • After planting God's Word in the hearts of people all over Guatemala and Mexico, Cameron Townsend (1896–1982) started Wycliffe Bible Translators so that all people could read the Good News for themselves. ISBN 1-57658-241-8

For a free catalog of books and materials contact
YWAM Publishing, P.O. Box 55787, Seattle, WA 98155
1-800-922-2143, www.ywampublishing.com

Heroes for Young Readers Activity Guides and CDs

by Renee Taft Meloche

Whether for home, school, or Sunday school, don't miss these fun-filled activity guides and CDs presenting the lives of other Heroes for Young Readers.

Heroes for Young Readers Activity Guides

For Books 1–4: Gladys Aylward, Nate Saint, Eric Liddell, George Müller • 1-57658-367-8
For Books 5–8: Amy Carmichael, Corrie ten Boom, Mary Slessor, William Carey • 1-57658-368-6
For Books 9–12: Betty Greene, David Livingstone, Adoniram Judson, Hudson Taylor • 1-57658-369-4

Heroes for Young Readers Activity Audio CD

Each activity guide has an available audio CD with book readings, songs, and fun activity tracks, helping you to get the most out of the Activity Guides!

CD for Books 1–4 • 1-57658-396-1
CD for Books 5–8 • 1-57658-397-X
CD for Books 9–12 • 1-57658-398-8

Heroes for Young Readers Activity Guide Package Special

Includes the activity guide, audio CD, and four corresponding Heroes for Young Readers hardcover books.

For Books 1–4 Package • 1-57658-375-9
For Books 5–8 Package • 1-57658-376-7
For Books 9–12 Package • 1-57658-377-5

Christian Heroes: Then & Now

by Janet and Geoff Benge

The Heroes for Young Readers books are based on the Christian Heroes: Then & Now biographies by Janet and Geoff Benge. Discover these exciting, true adventures for ages ten and up! Many unit study curriculum guides for older students are also available to accompany these biographies.

Gladys Aylward: The Adventure of a Lifetime • 1-57658-019-9
Nate Saint: On a Wing and a Prayer • 1-57658-017-2
Hudson Taylor: Deep in the Heart of China • 1-57658-016-4
Amy Carmichael: Rescuer of Precious Gems • 1-57658-018-0
Eric Liddell: Something Greater Than Gold • 1-57658-137-3
Corrie ten Boom: Keeper of the Angels' Den • 1-57658-136-5
William Carey: Obliged to Go • 1-57658-147-0
George Müller: The Guardian of Bristol's Orphans • 1-57658-145-4
Jim Elliot: One Great Purpose • 1-57658-146-2
Mary Slessor: Forward into Calabar • 1-57658-148-9
David Livingstone: Africa's Trailblazer • 1-57658-153-5
Betty Greene: Wings to Serve • 1-57658-152-7
Adoniram Judson: Bound for Burma • 1-57658-161-6
Cameron Townsend: Good News in Every Language • 1-57658-164-0
Jonathan Goforth: An Open Door in China • 1-57658-174-8
Lottie Moon: Giving Her All for China • 1-57658-188-8
John Williams: Messenger of Peace • 1-57658-256-6
William Booth: Soup, Soap, and Salvation • 1-57658-258-2
Rowland Bingham: Into Africa's Interior • 1-57658-282-5
Ida Scudder: Healing Bodies, Touching Hearts • 1-57658-285-X
Wilfred Grenfell: Fisher of Men • 1-57658-292-2
Lillian Trasher: The Greatest Wonder in Egypt • 1-57658-305-8
Loren Cunningham: Into All the World • 1-57658-199-3
Florence Young: Mission Accomplished • 1-57658-313-9
Sundar Singh: Footprints Over the Mountains • 1-57658-318-X
C.T. Studd: No Retreat • 1-57658-288-4

For a free catalog of books and materials contact
YWAM Publishing, P.O. Box 55787, Seattle, WA 98155
1-800-922-2143, www.ywampublishing.com